Mother's Song

Jacquelene Pearson

Mother's Song

Acknowledgements

'River farewell' and 'Homeland', in *Bird Before Landing*, Central Coast Poets Inc Anthology 2002

'Egg and spoon' and 'Portrait: middle age', in *Central Coast Poets Present Off the Path*, Australian Poetry, 2010

Thanks

Carl, Jess, Livy, Steve, Maryann, Central Coast Poets and Friday Night Poets – thanks for your love and nurturing.

Dedication

For Denise, Yelva, Miriam
and all the other mothers I have known

Mother's Song
ISBN 978 1 76109 339 5
Copyright © text Jacquelene Pearson 2022
Cover image: *Breathe in the keys*, by Stephen Pearson

First published 2022 by
GINNINDERRA PRESS
PO Box 3461 Port Adelaide 5015
www.ginninderrapress.com.au

Contents

Rivers We Cross

Cardiac care	11
Homeland	13
On the offensive	15
Fallujah	16
Blood	17
Rangoon	18
The disappeared	19
Soldiers I have known	20
River farewell	22
The Surprise	24
Solitary winters	26
Rivers we cross	28
Greste	30
Elders	31
Always will be	33
Beach fishing	35
Red pebble	36
One breath	37
Macquarie Fields	38
Headlines	39
Driving in Marrickville	40
War of notions	41
Dear Mr Thomas	42
Sister silence	43
Blackout poem	45
Soul food	46
Hello hack	47
Tan renga	48
Tanka	49

Cycling	50
Innocence	51
High tide	52
Telling the moon	53
From stone	54
Settler's clock	55
Perspective	56
Blue	58
River farewell II – Robby and ruby slippers	59

Bloom

Mending black holes	63
Hands	64
Silent war	66
Dear friend	67
Over dinner	69
Child	70
The dream	71
The cycle	72
It is the silences	74
This bed	75
Balm	76
The juggler	78
Fall in	79
Emmerson Street	80
The missing years	81
Jay	83
The telling	84
Sebastian	85
Image	86
17	87
My son	88

Pink	89
Sunrise	90
For a moment	91
Portrait: middle age	93
I'm 40	94
Courting the luthier	96
We	98
Egg and spoon	99
Mother's song	100
Central Coast girls	101
At three	102
I succumb	103
Window box	104
Kneading	105
Bloom	106
About the Poet	107

Rivers We Cross

Cardiac care

She is naked.
The male nurse lifts her tenderly
as he gives blood, takes blood,
gives pain, takes pain.
He asks her age but the agony's got her tongue
so he answers for her:
> *I can see you're minutes away from puberty.*
> *You're about to become a woman*
> *and soon you will be strong and well.*
> *I can see.*

She can see
both arms strapped to boards
two dark drainage tubes
at the base of her rib cage
to keep the fluid off her lungs.
They wired her breastbone back together.
Internal stitches and magic tape
keep the scar narrow.

Mummy says she is lucky
to have a new-model scar.
It only goes from neck to belly.
It doesn't curl around her back
like the old-fashioned ones.

Is it the pain or morphine
that makes her scream?
Makes her bed lumpy.
> *I'm lumpy.*

Covers her in spiders and snakes.
> *Get them off me. I'm all lumpy.*

The young priest sits with her
when Mummy takes a break.
His hand warms her cold fingers.
> *Would you like to pray?*

he asks quietly.
She obeys.
> *Our Father, who art in Heaven*
> *hallowed be thy name…*

Is he crying or watching?
She is eleven.

Homeland

She lives in the Village now.
Pays a pretty greenback
for an apartment with a view.
Just doesn't look at the wounds
where the towers used to stand.

Nine-eleven, she was there.
Fled to the street from the 30th floor.
Swept up in the steel and concrete storm.
Shrapnel gouged her shins
as she rode the human wave.

Now it's Christmas at Queenscliff.
Safe between the flags.
We glimpse her scars,
sense everything's changed.
    I don't like to go there
is all she'll say.

Still loves to shop,
earn the big bucks,
holiday in Tuscany,
date New York Italian boys.
Come home to us? Occasionally.

We always beg her to stay.
She does her usual round of friends,
family and favourite cafés.
Then she's off again.

We head back to the beach.
Sun-drunk we dive
and glide to the shore.
She flies north to winter
and the president's new war.

On the offensive

The president's speech
was saccharine sweet.
Old Dame Liberty
perched on his shoulder.
But behind those
pleading little eyes
a warmonger's
rage smouldered.

Fallujah

The saviours pursue her
like a virgin debutante
all white and right
for the victory parade.

The news footage unveils her
as a war-hardened whore.
All blood and mud.
For whose God
will she be saved?

Blood

A woman holds a child.
There is blood
on her hands.
She rocks.
She screams to the sky
restored to calm blue
seconds after turmoil.

Fire,
broken glass,
blood everywhere.
She rocks.
She bays – at the camera
into our living rooms.
So much blood.

Rangoon

i.

If priest, rabbi, imam
join your saffron march
if we all link hands in every land
to guide you safely past, surely then
we can silence the guns.

ii.

The holy rouge
drains from your cheeks.
You have your wish for silent streets.
Abandoned shoes tell of a crime.
Batons thrust into thin backs.
How many lost lives
does the body count hide?

iii.

Allies and foes chastise you
like an errant child.
But they have their own
misdemeanours to hide.
We are left to meditate
on the question of why
even the most holy
can never march as one.

The disappeared

Light, chemicals, film –
a weathered portrait without a frame
held between the farmer's fingers.
He walked, bare feet, from province to city
searching for shadows, traces.
Politicians promised but did not do their duty.
Their silence conspired.
The photo fades –
the father's face engraved with the grief
of his boy's evanescence.

According to the National Human Rights Commission, 2,240 were 'disappeared' in Nepal during its 13-year civil war between the Maoists and agitating political parties. Many believed they were killed in custody and buried in mass graves. Some parents gave up hope. Tika Kandel kept looking for his son.

Soldiers I have known

Alf, 1922–1999
Raised in those famous breadline years
you learned early how to fight for life.
Your family walked from Carlton to Port Kembla
picking fruit along the Murray
in newspaper shoes with string shoelaces.
It was an even longer journey
from the steelworks to the pyramids.
You never talked about the war
stayed out of the club on Anzac Day
at least until the two-up was under way.
Marched to your grave with nothing
but secrets pinned to your chest.

Spencer, 1925–2003
You marched straight out of your mother's
milking shed and onto a troop train
her forged signature in your pocket.
It was one big tropical dream until
you woke that morning, frozen under fire,
on a sweaty New Britain beach.
'Charge, for God's sake,' the sergeant yelled.
So you did. Was it the memory of the men
who met the end of your bayonet,
as much as of lost mates, that got you up
before dawn, for 50 years, in late April frosts
to pray? 'Lest we forget, best we forget.'

Rob 1927–2012
What did you see when, at seventeen,
you marched into Nagasaki?
No ricepaper houses, nor silk kimono,
Only silhouettes seared into concrete,
wounds that couldn't be lanced or dressed
nothing but walking ghosts to liberate.
You always kept your love for Japan quiet.
Quiet – that's how it left you –
patient and gentle all through your years.
Was that the message in your deathbed prayer?
'My god, my dream.' What did you see?

River farewell

Kingfishers herald the dawn
as I wash faces,
pack lunches,
tie shoelaces,
and wonder:

how many tiny fingers
did you guide with paper,
scissors and paint?
How many young minds
did you set ablaze
with that up-yours jaw
and dizzying gaze?

I sit by your beloved river
looking for a sign
to explain your pain and passing.
I search for your reflection
and find it there in mine.

I hold hands with strangers
bound by your memory.
Can you feel our embrace?
Hear our final words of friendship,
our salute to your colour and grace?

Your painting hangs on a new wall.
I can see it from my favourite chair.
It's a river shack.
You're standing there,
paintbrush in hand, staring
out across the land,
savouring the scene,
smiling down on me.

'No regrets,' I hear you sing.

The Surprise

what's left of her
is hidden in the mangroves
a whisper from the boardwalk
once a grand working girl
her lines a master's craft
from oak and pine
now she sits
belly sinking in the mud

the kids' summer hideaway
climb her ropes
stand on her bridge
command great adventures
sneaking home at sunset
black mud from toe to neck

a descendant
took up residence
unwelcome in town
she became his fortress
the only family member
still prepared to give sanctuary

the police
found stolen goods
labelled him a felon
dragged him through the mangroves
drove him from the river

the village
turned its back on both
too much mud
it sticks you know
tides change
secrets keep
in silence
he is gone
she is there,
still, a whisper

Solitary winters

Check behind the bedhead for last year's red wine stain
chuckle with relief to find it cleaned away –
no expulsion from paradise for that one night
of hedonism and a rickety bedhead.

Flop into deckchairs and scan the horizon
for that familiar cluster of islands
see where the tides have carved
fresh canyons into the estuary.

Our morning ritual begins:
squeeze into wetsuits
tiptoe across icy sand
throw tired bodies into the waves.

At low tide the beach is a gallery.
The wet sand a canvas
stretched between rocky points.
Soldier crab diggings are dragonflies
and flowers in the local style.

Flying foxes cloak the sky
as the full moon takes hold of the tide
to coax a chain of silver
waves along the creek.

Knee deep in a shadowy pool
a silent plover waits
patient as a statue for the current
to catch his evening meal.

No ochre sunrise stirs us today.
Sea mist turns the horizon to steel grey.
Time to pack for home.
Watch the waves dissolve our presence.
Pleased we will not leave a stain.

Rivers we cross

We kick off our shoes as we cross the Hunter;
it's time to think about gypsy skirts and caravans
even though we are only towing a trailer.

At the Manning I pause to think of a childhood friend.
One of these years I will turn in to Taree
and knock on her door.

The Hastings makes me grieve for nieces and a nephew
not seen for years. I look for their baby faces
but strangers fill the streets of Port.

We rent a little boat for a morning
and share the Nambucca
with dolphins and sea eagles.

As we reach the Bellinger we start to prepare
for what might lie ahead.
The Clarence and Richmond roll by

without a glance as we focus
on how they will be
what they will need this year.

At the Tweed we pause before turning into their street
to hope we find them at work in the garden
or sipping tea on the back veranda.
They are well but frail when we arrive
and we vow not to leave it so long
to make the journey next time.

In a quiet moment she takes my hand
and tells me of her fears:
> *Sometimes when he falls asleep in his chair*
> *it's like he completely leaves his body, it's empty.*
> *He just isn't there any more. I can't look away*
> *until I see him move or breathe.*
> *And I know one day he won't come back.*

I squeeze her hand, find something comforting to say
knowing that, in two days, we will be gone with the tide.

Greste

Some men can stay free
even when locked
in the darkest cave.
They still see starlight
hear the ocean's wave song,
smell the damp
of dawn and dusk,
even when bonded,
silenced and blind.

His words were our lens
on the world. Through him
we shared the anguish
and strain of those living
in the cesspit of war.
Even from those torn
and gutted states –
and then from prison's cage –
his voice carried enough truth
to keep us in the light.

Now truly free
may he long feel
the sands of peace
beneath his feet.

Elders

The nights are cold at Docker River
but there are no carers to keep
the elders safe while they sleep
and now a name we no longer speak
lies in a grave we won't remember.

She was a child when the missionaries came:
taught to dress, taught to pray,
taught to speak a certain way,
not to wander, but to stay.
White law, whitewash, white way.

Nothing white about the night
she fell into the open pit
where the elders came to sit
for comfort from night's frigid bite
until the staff returned at daylight.

The memory sits as a lump in his throat.
Tufts of down filled the air
as flames engulfed her skin and hair
and still she kept standing there
in her melting sky-blue coat.

If only he had let her burn
not made her live through the pain
of nine hours by road and plane
a journey to Darwin made in vain
from which she did not return.

The nights are cold in Docker River.
Still there are no carers to keep
the elders safe while they sleep.
Sorry is a word easy to speak;
action not so easy to deliver.

When Dulcy Brumby died from burns at a Docker River aged care facility, the ABC revealed we have two systems of aged care in Australia. One for whites and one for First Nations elders. Neither is good enough.

Always will be

I know you watch me
as I peg my washing
or dig in the garden.
You send me signs:

a brown snake
under the wash line
was my favourite.
Mocking laughter
echoed through the bush
as I poked it with a stick
and squirmed
when the maggots fell out.

Some days I think
I feel your breath
on my shoulder.
When I turn
there is a feather
tinted blue
and the breeze
from your departure.

I know you watch
because this is your land.
The kookaburra is your eyes.
The late-night crickets
your clapping sticks.
I wish I could join
your dance.

For now I will plant
callistemon –
pansies and sweet william
don't like the sandy soil –
knowing each bloom
and birdsong
confirms me
as the visitor
and this
as your land.

Beach fishing

Brazen wind slaps cheeks.
Waves lick bare legs.
Creep up denim to create
human high-water mark.
Tide is turning.

Silver flash catches eye.
Feet buried where they stand.
Listen to the reel spin.
Journey with line and hook.
Moon is fading.

Hours drift.
Mind floats out with tide.
Empty bucket tells story.
Casting practice, shoulders shrug.
Sun starts searing.

Retrace footprints through dunes.
Plant kiss on sleeping lips.
Searching eyes survey the catch.
Where's breakfast? Grinning retort.
Silver flash still swimming.

Red pebble

Veins through blood.
Torn flesh
washed smooth.
Shoved and tumbled,
sand-cut, sundried
and salt-cured.
In my pocket:
curio, object of beauty.
Tomorrow, on my walk
I will find company for it.
I will thread each piece
into a string of beads
to add fresh meaning
to time-worn
tales of life
with the sea.

One breath

At spring's low tide they made boys
wade waist deep to gather shells
until the beds of Baldwin Creek
were stripped bare of their silk sheets.

Then traps of rum were set
to snare the young Njul Njul men
for unlike the whites, on just one breath,
they could bring shell from the sea's depths.

Boys took the poison and woke with bound hands
in the darkness and stench of the lugger's hold
but even then the bounty from a single breath
couldn't sate their masters' lust for shelled gold.

So natives and imports trussed in canvas suits
weighed down with metal boots and bells
were dragged along the seabed from dawn to dark
raw strength and pride their lifeline.

Some would last a month – the heroes survived six.
Some of the shell was even used
to pave the streets of Broome
until a 60s council buried the evidence with tonnes of tar
perhaps to cover the scar
and silence the telling of the pearl divers' story.

Macquarie Fields

Mothers and aunts get no time to grieve
as troopers storm with shield and club
to restore order to Poverty's Fields.

Soweto? Belfast?
Any town where ignorance
is left to infect
one generation to the next.

Across the Harbour the self-made lament
their taxes wasted on handouts
                       just shoot the bloody lot,
they insist.

The young rise with stones and flames.
Headlines make them infamous for a day
until the public's attention strays.

Jackboots prevail. Spirits cannot take flight
when hopes are ground down
to take root in the dust of poverty's fields.

Headlines

In Melbourne, the man who threw
his daughter off the Westgate Bridge
was sentenced to life in prison today.
It happened on her first day of school.
Witnesses said she didn't make a sound
the whole way down.

In Perth, the community wants to know why
teenage drunken violence is getting worse.
So the government has decided to pay
for research to test whether it's safe
to mix spirits with energy drinks.

In Fukushima, the nuclear plant workers
keep trying to plug holes, stem the flow
through each aftershock.
There's nothing higher than level seven –
nothing to eat but local fish and vegetables.

At my house, the latest generation
of bush turkey makes its daily trek
across the roof span, along the tightrope
perimeter fence, through the dry creek
bed to the mound just as its forebears
have done for thousands of years.

Driving in Marrickville

you stand
on the yellow lines
waiting
until it is safe to cross

I stop
smile
and wave
for you to walk

you hesitate
and I am ashamed
to see fear and mistrust
on your silk-framed face

we're both
someone's daughter
perhaps sisters or mothers
sharing the same land

but within
the politics of terror
the road beneath us
cracks and divides

War of notions

We've moved on from Roses,
progressed from Nations.
Now we're so evolved
we wage wars against Notions:
like Drugs
and Crime
and let's not forget Terror.
It's a bit of a shame
that for all our greatness,
we haven't learned
how to fight the Heinous:
like Famine
or Disease
or our truest of enemies:
Selfishness and Greed.

Dear Mr Thomas

It is a sullen art
this thing that gets inside my head
repeats, refines each line
while I stare at the ceiling
until I coalesce – allow it to drag
me, pencil in hand, to a desk
at the other end of the house
to turn the back of yesterday's
shopping list into a tract
cross-hatched with ever-darker
patches of black skepticism
until with on last orgasmic
exhalation it is there, said and done
and a wink of sun
through the back window
keeps my sleepless secret.

A response to 'In my craft or sullen art' – Dylan Thomas

Sister silence

at 51 she told a stranger
about that day
when she was six
and the school doctor
held her back
and the sky turned black

at 51 talking for hours
cleaned out decades
of guilt and shame
she felt fresh air hit
the bottom of her lungs
for the first time
in decades

at 51 no more rabbit holes
no more good girl potions
no more evil eve
no more women-are-wicked
-witches-of-the-west
-world view
just this moment and love
and her true self

at 51 she still asked why
not why it happened
but why no one noticed
and why it still
happens somewhere
to someone every day
and why she still wakes
to that ghostly breath
on her neck
in the darkness

Blackout poem

in the future
on an assassination mission
a kung fu master
whose wedding is spoiled
by a posse of gangsters
falls out of love
and gets sidetracked
the problem is his heart
requires violence

Soul food

the city gave her
psychic salmonella
so one Friday night
she drove north
pitched her tent
in a Swansea caravan park
and shaved her head
in the communal shower block

back at her desk
Monday morning
she told anyone who asked
she'd done it for charity

Hello hack

Pardon me
for entering
your world
where bastardry
and bullshit hold
the balance of power.
Where answers
must be limited
to a single sheet
of well-rehearsed
talking points
and one must never
turn the page
to contemplate
the how or why
nor walk into a street
and dare to meet
a person who has not
been polled or screened
one of those you work
so hard to keep
uncomfortably dumb
so the power
and control
rests in the laps
of humanity's
very least profound.

Tan renga

I fell in love
with the wings of birds
the light of spring on them
sliced through black winter thoughts
raised my sights for new journeys

Tanka

tiny birds flit
across wetland lily pads
they walk on water
like lotus-pink mini gods
to bring me nature's teachings

Cycling

At dawn
the water laps and folds
like a silk sheet in the breeze.
It mirrors the sailing boat mast
as a corkscrew –
> *there are no straight lines in nature.*

I follow the water's edge
through the musty mangroves
toward the opening eyelids of day,
swerving to miss other early risers –
> *if it is to be it is up to me.*

My right pedal flies off.
I feebly try to screw it back on
when a stranger appears with a spanner.
At least you're not hurt, he says –
> *never be too proud to ask for help.*

This track carries a human procession
like those biology diagrams:
from pert girl to sagging matron;
from zesty jogger to zimmer frame –
> *for everything turn, turn, turn…*

From the first thread of DNA
to the arc of dirt sprayed
by a grave digger's spade
around we go
around and around –
> *and where we'll stop, nobody knows.*

Innocence

from earth's core
through the soles of her feet
she feels it
in birdsong, wind chime
beat and rhythm
sweet humming melody
heartbeat rising

High tide

Here she comes
silk petticoats trilling
like a dancing bride.
She throws back her gold
and lapis covers, raises
bare white shoulders and arms
to embrace, one more time,
her suitors on the shore.

One lick from her kissy-curled tongue
can cause canyons to fall to the depths
of the dark bed that spawned her.
Weeds, shells, green and silver threads
are pulled along in the train of her gown
to be left scattered on the dance floor
at dawn when, without sound, she retreats.

Still gasping from her touch,
as the sky moves
from flamingo to blue,
the suitors wait, counting the hours,
until they can reach for the hand
of the next waltzing virgin.

Telling the moon

Dear friend,
tonight a full-cheeked moon
entices each wave all the way
to the dunes. It is her gift –
as ancient as the scars
on her face. She has seen ice melt
and mountains fall, remaining stoic.
Her timeless telling still radiates.
> *Until we truly learn to kneel,*
> *how can we learn to live in grace?*

From stone

you have invented my soul
bisected sight from emptiness
to sharpen your axe
I lie down with you
my wounded skull's spilled
blood and bone catch fire
and we are head dressed
pelvis   breasts
press   press
you rise up
to pull me in
take me below
this fragile remnant
down through sand and stone
to join your night dance

Settler's clock

Bird song
the best alarm.
A cheerful way to face
the day before man-made noise
takes over our senses
and enslaves our brains.
And then, as the washing comes in,
we notice it again –
soothing birdsong.

Perspective

i.

He says it may surprise her to know
he sees the world in black and white.
She raises an eyebrow, curls her lip,
and he knows she knows.
He says colour is about perspective:
>*Look at that grass*
>*I used to see only green*
>*but look, you can see*
>*yellow, black, shadows and layers.*

Colour, he says, is about technique
about seeing all the shades
and spaces in between.
He must learn that, he says,
and he knows she knows.

ii.

They're on the *African Queen*.
She Hepburn, he Bogart.
(It's a fifty-dollar hire boat on the Bucca River.)
She navigates. No problems upstream –
green markers to the right, red to the left.
Drop anchor to fish and picnic.
The downstream journey should be easy –
red right, green left, but she loses the plot
ends up in the shallows, almost causes Bogart
to rip off his shirt and dive in with the mud crabs.
The hire boat man is pacing on the shore.
> *You're supposed to come back*
> *the way you went up.*
> *See that marker, rocks under there.*
> *Now sit down and swing*
> *your legs over the side.*
> *Take the easy way out.*

Bogart gives the old bugger a wink.
She has no chance
to regain her Katie composure.

iii.

Everything is tinted green.
She wonders: will she ever see
the rose-colour part
of this 3D movie.

Blue

cloudy morning
sun glows red
then hides
and the sky
is sheeted grey
except for one
circle of blue
above them
on the empty beach

River farewell II – Robby and ruby slippers

She wore red shoes
to his wake;
ruby red, soft leather,
to honour their short
but succulent love.

He was a wild boy.
Wiped out his boat
on a bridge pylon
in full view of the island
named after his grandfather.
His dog was still tethered
when they raised the boat.
That's how they knew
it was an accident.

His young brother
did doughnuts
through the graveyard
'Bad to the Bone' blaring
out the windows of his ute.
He'd shaved lightning bolts
into the sides of his head
to honour their short
but brutal bond.

And at the wake
he passed out on a table
at the back of the pub;
freaked out the local kids
who thought it was Robby
lying in state.

And at the wake
she spoke softly
of their plans
to live on the river.
They were moving in
that weekend.
Softly she spoke
back and forth
she rocked
in her ruby Mary Janes
to honour his short
dance with life.

Bloom

Mending black holes

black
under fingernails
charcoal eyes
breath in the dark

one day
you will bury him
there will be frost
on the ground
and you will dance
barefoot
until your feet are blue
to farewell the pain

bury it
sever the suffering
it ends with you
leave it there
let it lie
in that dark space
carry the child
forward to daylight

Hands

walk the beach
sit on the break wall
wait
to be noticed
as his hands play
with the line

flowers
telegrams
always and forever
more and more
every day
he works shifts
she stays home
alone

the girl
in the flat upstairs
tops herself
her insides bleed
through the floor
to stain
their ceiling
the stench
fills the building
they carry her out
in a body bag

Indian silk
French lace
a horse-drawn carriage
she will make it work
a bigger flat
a baby boy

he comes home at dawn
smeared lipstick
smoke and booze
and perfume and sorry
more and more
forever and ever

hands hold hands beg
hands pray hands touch
hands slap hands push
hands hide say sorry
for ever and ever
hands wave goodbye

Silent war

Sometimes she still feels like that girl
in the back room of the corner shop –
the one who made everyone laugh;
the one forever stuck on level 13
of the Space Invader machine.
That girl is the one she loves:
to piggyback; together they skate
and dance and giggle at the world.

Sometimes she still feels like that skinny,
sickly schoolgirl –
the one who got pushed into the boys' loos;
the one afraid of drowning in the shallow end
of the local War Memorial Pool.
That girl is the one she hates:
that ear-chewing shrew she struggles
to keep out of her grown up space.

Sometimes she still feels like that helpless girl
in the darkness. The one who didn't know
it was OK to say no –
the one forever screaming
in the silence of that childhood tomb.

That girl is the one she needs:
to love and hold and grow
or she will always be stuck on level 13
drowning in the shallow end
screaming in the silence.

Dear friend

Do you remember our place in Hill Street?
The neighbours thought we were running a brothel:
paisley curtains flapping out the top window
in the westerly. Open-all-hours cars in the drive;
malnourished young men dropping in to be fed –
food and fanny always on the menu.

I remember the night you cooked sausages
that tasted like shit in my mouth.
I felt buried alive. Ran downstairs
to the phone booth across the street
weeping for my mother who did not answer.

Your new friends called you a coconut
for keeping your white mates. They were right.
I did betray you. Searched your room,
confiscated the razor blades
you were using to exorcise your bleached childhood.

I slammed doors in your face – callow youth
blinded me to your grieving. You made me
promise never to write your story
but the truth still sits like shit in my mouth.

From Hill Street I followed some bloke to a farmhouse
you moved to the hostel. I visited once
but felt like the enemy. You didn't graduate
but came to our ceremony – the photo
shows you smiling but clinging to my arm.

We met twice when you move to Redfern.
The last time under a fig tree in the Gardens.
We drank champagne. You with your new lover.
Me with my baby and shiny ring.
Then 20 years of silence – no calls or letters returned
not even a response to our ad in the *Koori Mail*.

I hope you have peace, that you still write and paint.
I hope your laughter still peels paint from walls.
I've lost other friends but you were the treasure
I threw away. I hope you'll understand why
I can't keep my silence.
I can't sit and watch the troops move in, 'to protect the children',
without yelling for the truth to be told
starting with mine, here on this page.
I was the problem and, too late, I am sorry.

Over dinner

you nudge the lip of her glass
she invites you to pour
she sups on your attention
while I thirst for times
when such gestures
were my preserve

the silent drive home
leaves me choking
on loneliness

Child

His cold back
makes her turn
to the child.
Nose to nose,
forehead to
forehead, she
drinks in
the innocence
discarded
long ago.

Broken doll waits
at the bottom
of her toy box.

The dream

He dreams they're happy.
Embracing at sunrise.
Building sandcastles.
Laughing with their children.

He wakes to the alarm.
Cold house in darkness.
Her cold shoulder reminds him
they are not quite living the dream.

The cycle

Screw you:
for sucking me back
through the crack
into the victim vacuum;

for parking your shoes
under my bed
then scratching your head
when I ask you
to lie in it with me;

for slapping the smile
off my face
then retreating
to your safe place
when it's time
to administer pain relief;

for stepping over
my grief
when you find me
crumpled
at the bottom
of your stairway to heaven;

for emptying
each available bottle
before you feebly slink
through the door
to kneel in front of me
and concede
that I have every right
to say
screw you.

It is the silences

she cannot breach nor fathom.
They are dead seas.
They are lost babies.
They are cutting insults
even if unintended.

What should she say
to the waiter
who asks why
she left half her mains?

They are dough in a hot oven.
They expand to fill all available space.
They take over,
tie tongues, until
there is nothing left to say.

This bed

This bed is like a brick.
It makes my bones ache.
I ache even more
now your side is empty.
I haven't ventured over there
since you left.

This bed is where
we made our babies
and the promise
to write our own story.
Now I grieve for our
egg and spoon mornings.

It is winter. Every day
the pre-dawn chill wakes me
but still, I am not prepared
to leave this bed.

Balm

suck my brain out
through my third eye
take it in your hands
like putty to mould
finally
into your preferred shape
cut my tongue out
with your wit
hold it
above your head
a trophy
finally
my silence
your preferred state

Or

rub my shoulders
lift my hair
to kiss my neck
run me a bath
and wash my back
savour the stillness
at the end of the day
let your lips
find my cheek
let our passion
be your drink
be my strength
my balm
against the blues
take my hand
and lead me
through the darkness
to our bed

The juggler

The juggler needs a rest
from her double life
as journalistic genius
and charming earth-mother wife.

Each day a delirious wasteland
of broken deadlines and dribble.
Please take one of her orbs away
before she takes a tumble.

She's truly thankful to the Sisters
for their bra-burning revolution.
It just hasn't given her
an enduring solution.

Working past seven again.
It really makes her think.
She helps pay the mortgage
but still has her arms in his sink.

To be honest, there are days
when her tired soul sings
to be shackled, for a little while,
in grandmother's apron strings.

Is anybody listening?
The juggler needs a rest.

Fall in

it was years since she'd been
        to the march
the year her mother was dying
she'd stood in the sleet
with a flimsy umbrella
shielding the skin and bones
of her truest love
        There's hardly any of them left now:
        a handful from World War Two;
        a dozen from Vietnam;
        and it's all over.
but she is still that little girl
fingers engulfed by mother's hand
standing to attention at the cenotaph
a sprig of rosemary pinned over her heart
in the dress reserved for Sunday Communion.
        Lest we forget,
        lest we forget.
so how did she get here
in this dwindling crowd
with all these ghosts
how did she become
the next in line
to be remembered?

Emmerson Street

Stand on the front veranda
ribs pressed against the railing
take in the languid town below
church spires, streets where creeks once ran.
Slink into the wicker chair
surrounded by maiden's hair and chain of hearts.
The front door will stick when you turn the key –
free it with a nudge of the hip.
Open the piano lid and breathe in the keys.
Fumble through 'Amazing Grace'
and recall mother's passion for Chopin.
Walk to the kitchen where the kettle will be hissing
on the wood-fired stove – there will be Arnott's Assorted Creams with tea
or SAOs with tomato and cheese if you are royalty.
Walk down the hall and bend like and overgrown Alice
to use the little handle – a cotton reel
painted and nailed to assist one hundred years
of tiny hands searching for mother, nanna or mamma
in the back garden – follow the path past the fernery
and under the peppercorn trees – help yourself
to strawberries, snow peas, or fill your skirt
with loquats – remember to admire the gladioli –
the number of blooms, assortment of colours.
Leave by the driveway – if you go back
through the house you might start to wake ghosts
need to explain visits not made, time not spent
before they passed.

The missing years

The family
preserved their infant smiles
in polished frames
and pressed in books;
birth dates recorded, remembered
gifts dispatched
to the last known address.

The mother
ripped them away
to move north
with another man.
She took the furniture.
He wore the debt.
He never
could have done enough.

The father
took his expensive court orders
to her door
every second weekend and holiday.
She sent him away
with empty arms.
His tongue turned to stone.

The rage
made him sick for years.
He forgot how to think.
Slowly he built
a new life
from the shards she left,
but never, ever quite the same.

The children?
They grow, learn,
laugh and cry, love and hate
without him.
He wants to believe
they will seek him out
so they can all reclaim
a fraction of the missing years.

Jay

only ever wanted to be Action Man
rode his motorbike too fast
fell in love like it was a rescue mission
still carries a photo of the best friend
who died when they were both about ten

when he calls too often or doesn't call at all
it's the first sign he's riding too fast again
he talks about coming home to an empty house
about his kids calling another man dad
he talks   but cannot define
the unbearable weight of his emptiness

so sometimes when the black seeps in
he breaks every promise made in therapy
and speeds off to join his old mate Action Man

The telling

she sat in the darkness
alone with her demons
alone with her memories
fractured   unseemly
and she thought   in the morning
she would do her telling

they'd drive to the water
let the waves touch their bare feet
like they had when children
and the sunlight would glisten
and he would listen
to her darkest remembering

and where it would take them
she'd no way of knowing
like clay worked through fingers
that becomes cloudy water
as hands are rinsed clean

the weight kept her weeping
alone in the darkness
for she knew   in the morning
she must do her telling

Sebastian

What should a Great Aunt do
when you come to my door
on your young mother's hip,
sodden nappy, grubby fists?
Feed you apple and arrowroot,
show you the bunny, open the cubby,
watch you swing and climb and kick,
notice you have my brother's brow.

I want to keep you, so I can teach you
colours and numbers and words –
like love and home and safe –
but I can't change what has gone before
or fix what hasn't happened yet.
So I gently wash your hands and face
and send you away
with a sandwich in a snaplock bag
and a promise to pray you are safe.

When I was a little girl
Great Uncles and Aunts would visit.
My favourite would give me
a shiny silver coin – to keep –
I cannot remember his name.

Image

I've kept some photos for our son.
One of you posing like Popeye on the *Achille Lauro*.
The two of us know what went on below
in the honeymoon stateroom where we lay

the foundations for the tortuous union
between your spite and my self-doubt.
You tell him you are divorcing again.
I find him weeping – for you, for himself,

for his half-brother and stepmother
who you will be leaving.
I tell him you're a good man, just weak
and indecisive. Perhaps if I had been wiser

I could have stayed and made you stronger.
Angrily he tells me his greatest fear
is that even in your absence
he grows in your image.

17

I have rinsed the clay from my hands
switched off the wheel. He is out of the kiln
cooling his heels, before he decides
which road to follow, the journey to take
that is sure to add fresh layers of colour and glaze.

I plan to stay around for as long as I can
to fill cracks and repair broken bits
but when you say he is too young to catch the train
to your place, or ask who will teach him to drive
when he already has his P-plates, you testify
to the calls you didn't make, the football games
you didn't watch him play, fevers you didn't medicate.

And what could have been your reprieve?
Was it that I decided to leave?

Now he sees your tears as your own father
prepares to die. There's one thing left to say.
Hurry, embrace him,
before you leave that too late.

My son

Your absence is
the misspoken
misdeeds
of a mother
drowning
an unclocking tick
a quaking
unearthed.
And if this regret
could be a mound
of soil
in my hands
I would work
day-night-day
for all of time
to render
a new path
between
our hearts.

Pink

decades ago
I lived pink
– hot   baby   pink
knickers   socks   PJs
bedroom walls   sheets
dolls clothes, cot, stroller
lunch box, library bag…
ham it up
go exclusively hot –
raincoat, patent leather brogues,
lipstick…
kick the habit girl
graduate to red –
that's another story.

Sunrise

as a young woman
she roared back
at the waves
feet sinking at the shoreline
waiting for her sunrise

For a moment

He loved her:
her slight form
dancing the rim
of the rink.
His music box ballerina
all tulle and lip gloss
and promise.

He loved her:
with loyalty
until she left
him behind
for college boys
behind his white
picket fence
that never
could have
kept her home.

They loved her:
those college boys.
She collected
their virginities
in labelled jars
and failed to notice
how petrified
they were of her
appetite.

He loved her:
enough to bring forth
a perfect boy child
to teach her
the burdensome bliss
of the unconditional.
Not enough
to cast out
the demons
of lifetimes past.

He loved her:
at first
with writhing pain
and blame
until time and faith
and hope
tamed those demons
and gave them peace
at least for a moment.

Portrait: middle age

One day her heart falls out.
She tries to catch it
between her knees
but it rolls in the dirt
and can't be cleaned

or put back in.
A jelly in the dust
outside a lolly shop:
her mouth waters
for opportunities lost.
She works at the stains

on her palms with a tissue.
They turn old-blood brown
not scarlet or ruby.
There is no fire engine
left in her lips.

And with her heart gone
other organs go out in sympathy.
Her spine curls
like a dreaming snake.
Strength is a vapour
lost with each
exhalation.

I'm 40

Does that mean I should start
acting like a proper lady?
Cut my hair short? Replace my
Lennon sunnies with dark,
rectangular frames?
Adopt raw silk and linen as my habit?
Lunch in better restaurants
with the right crowd?
Or should I revert to the 'up yours'
asymmetrical cuts of my teens?
Paint-smattered T-shirts with stretchy
purple skirts and pink patent leather
lace-ups? Rejoin the revolution?
Free Palestine? Now that sounds
like a thankless job.

No more babies for me. That hurts.
The urge is strong. Mind and hormones
willing; body lagging behind and I did
marry that older man. I will allow myself
a couple of years to let go. Keep helping
my three beauties to grow.

Have I found it? Your desert oasis.
Fed by an ancient underwater river.
All around the searing heat snaps at my ankles,
fills my mouth with bitter red dust,
but here, my new wings will have time to dry.
They are grand. Azure and black.
There are cool ponds with water
so clear they project images
of surrounding rocks and palms.
I have learned to swim and, soon, I will fly.

Courting the luthier

Brush by his desk
on the way to the tearoom.
Inhale pheromone tones
mixed with notes of leather and soap.

Pause on your return to ask
of his weekend and take
a sneak peak
at those slender fingers,

tanned hands,
manicured cuticles,
nails cut straight
except for the one

he keeps long and strong
for Sunday plucking.
Imagine as you walk away
you are his favourite instrument:

old growth planed to hourglass;
firm body strung tight;
rubbed and oiled to shine.
One arm supports your neck

your torso languid
across his knees
shaded by his chest.
Cool blue eyes admire your form.

His elbow rests upon your hip.
Each stroke
across your belly
takes you closer

to singing out
for God
as together you search
for that sacred chord.

We

A continuum.
The perfect complement.
Black and white – left and right.
So when our time
is spent,
when the last tree
is ready to fall,
two halves shall join
at nature's command
and we will stay.
Complete.

Egg and spoon

when her head fits under his chin
his arms embrace her breasts and neck

when her back is pressed against
his chest   his loins a nest for her hips

when at rest they take the fold and form
the delicate strength   of a paper bird

then she knows
what it is like to fly

Mother's song

My essence
and goodness
the rose
in your
cheek.

My giving
maternal
your plump
little
grin.

Skin touching
hands kneading
I rock
you to
sleep.

Central Coast girls

I pack carefully for our day at the beach:
broad-brimmed hats and sun cream;
buckets and spades in your favourite Barbie bag.
I strap you in to your safe-n-sound as you chirp on
about sandcastles and seaweed.

At a red light we stop next to an old Holden.
A bikini-clad girl sits on the front seat.
The driver's hand embraces her shoulder.
Fake tan gives her a milk chocolate glow.
Plump lashes flutter and succumb to sun-induced sleep.

In my rear-vision mirror tiny fingers twirl blonde locks.
Your eyelids dance through a landscape of dreams
and I count the years, before you'll drive off,
in search of the big breaks
with your own tattooed sun god.

At three

You make old ladies laugh aloud.
I catch them sneaking you waves
and winks and raising fingers
to their lips to stifle giggles
as they share your mischief.
Do they, through the cobwebbed
chronicles of life, still remember
their own childhood antics?
Do you remind them of daughters
long grown and disappeared?
Or can even old ovaries feel
the undeniable tug of maternity?

I succumb

to the intoxicating completeness
of maternal love. Our lashes entangle
as they make the close-open-close
sweep to sleep. My lips press
against the silken back of your tiny fist
as you suck your thumb.
Your fingers weave through my hair.
Your toes nudge my hip. We breathe
as if still relying on one set of lungs.

Shh, shh, slowly you drift
and I wish you the sweetest
sweetest dreams.

Window box

Through the window
I watch her pick my flowers
I am scornful –
until I hear her calling
    these are for you, mummy

he is tall now
he bends to kiss my forehead
his hugs echo –
of my dear little boy
and love lost

kingfishers
start each day with a chorus
fresh and crisp –
like a spray of blossoms
in a spring window box

tiny birds
with God-like plumage
walk on water –
or skilfully flit
over wetland lily pads

Kneading

Cool butter on my fingertips
turns to silken sand
as it mixes with the flour
to remind me of the beach.

January sun on my shoulders.
Easterly breeze in my face.
Sand under fingernails
as I dig down, deep
to where it is cool and dark
and the water seeps in.

In this kitchen, in this home we've built,
not brick-by-brick, but year-by-year,
I want to take our girls
down to the shoreline
help them to dig deep
to reach that cool, dark place
and mix new flesh with old earth.

Bloom

as the bloom fades and in my heart
there is pain for two unborn
17 and 21 by now   no faces or names
just rainy hospital days   rough dates
and a quiet ache

to the three who stayed
the times I didn't play
or story tell or tightly hold
too tired   too career
too chasing the needs of the male
one teen survived   two left to guide

brightly unfolding buds those two
in my young image but shinier
in my voice but louder
in my skin but safer
born from richer soils in better times
robust and ready to thrive

as my bloom fades and in my heart
there is joy for three born and grown
tall troubadour, dancing faerie, monkey jester
thrive   be bright   look for light and colour
spin words to silk   leave darkness behind
and old ways to wilt   return to nurture earth
with my fading bloom

About the Poet

Jacquelene Pearson has been a professional writer for thirty-five years. Her favourite genre are investigative journalism and poetry. Her work is driven by her commitment to the importance of truth in the public interest and the need for greater levels of social and environmental justice. She hopes her work empowers individuals and communities to aspire to higher levels of accountability, equity and human decency. She has written poetry since she was about six years old. This is her first collection, with poems selected from the period 2000 to 2020.

www.ingramcontent.com/pod-product-compliance
Lightning Source LLC
Chambersburg PA
CBHW071126130526
44590CB00056B/2451